Science Vocabulary Readers

Super Spiders

Jason Blake

SCHOLASTIC INC.

NEW YORK • TORONTO • LONDON • AUCKLAND • SYDNEY
MEXICO CITY • NEW DELHI • HONG KONG • BUENOS AIRES

ISBN: 0-439-87638-9

Photo Credits

Cover: © Bill Beatty/Visuals Unlimited; title page: © John Cancalosi/DRK Photo; contents page, top: © James Rowan/DRK Photo; contents page, middle: © Anthony Bannister/Photo Researchers; contents page, bottom: © Bill Beatty/Visuals Unlimited; page 4: © James Rowan/DRK Photo; page 5: © Dr. William Weber/Visuals Unlimited; page 6, top: © Dwight Kuhn; page 6, bottom: © Dwight Kuhn; page 7: © John Mitchell/Photo Researchers; page 8: © Anthony Bannister/Photo Researchers; page 9: © Bill Beatty/Visuals Unlimited; page 10: © Dan Suzio/Photo Researchers; page 11: © Joe McDonald/DRK Photo; page 12: © Simon Pollard/Photo Researchers; page 13: © Bill Beatty/Visuals Unlimited; page 14: © Gary Meszaros/Visuals Unlimited; page 15: © Dwight Kuhn; back cover: © Michael Ederegger/DRK Photo.

Photo research by Amla Sanghvi
Design by Holly Grundon

12 11 10 9 8   9 10 11/0

Printed in the U.S.A.
First printing, September 2006

Contents

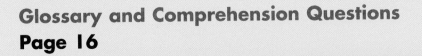

Chapter 1

What Is a Spider?

Spiders are creepy. Spiders are crawly.
They are also very cool!

Fun Fact

Spiders belong to an animal group called arachnids (a-**rak**-nids).

Spiders have been around for a long time. They were even alive in the time of dinosaurs!

Spiders have two body parts.

Insects have three body parts.

Spiders are not insects. How are they different? Their bodies have two parts. Insect bodies have three parts.

Here is another difference. Insects have six legs. Spiders have eight legs.

Chapter 2

Spider Senses

Two eyes are on the sides.

Most spiders have four pairs of eyes. Add that up and you get eight eyes! Even so, spiders don't see very well.

Fun Fact

Spiders use tiny hairs on their legs to hear and taste, too.

Spiders don't have noses or ears. They smell through little holes in their legs.

This is silk.

What else makes spiders special? They make **silk**. Silk is superstrong. Many spiders use it to spin webs.

A spider can eat 2,000 bugs in a year.

A lot of spiders use their sticky webs to catch flies and moths. Sometimes they wrap the bugs in silk to snack on later.

Chapter 3

So Many Spiders

Fun Fact

The goliath spider is so big it can eat a bird!

There are about fifty thousand kinds of spiders in the world. Most spiders are small, but a few are very big. This one is the size of a dinner plate.

Some spiders are bright colors. That allows them to crawl on flowers to hide. Can you spot the **crab spider** on this yellow flower?

Baby spiders are called spiderlings.

Some spiders take care of their babies.
This mother **wolf spider** carries them
on her back.

Fun Fact

Jumping spiders can jump 50 times the length of their bodies.

Some spiders can jump very far. You might even find this kind in your own backyard. Take a look!

Glossary

arachnids (a-**rak**-nids): a group of animals with eight legs including spiders, ticks, mites, and scorpions

crab spider (**crab spye**-dur): this kind of spider has two legs that look like crab claws

goliath spider (go-**lie**-eth **spye**-dur): this tarantula is the biggest spider alive

jumping spider (**juhmp**-ing **spye**-dur): this kind of spider jumps from place to place

silk (**silk**): a strong, thin thread made by spiders

spiderlings (**spye**-dur-**lings**): baby spiders

wolf spider (**wulf spye**-dur): this kind of spider is hairy like a wolf

Comprehension Questions

1. Can you name one way that spiders are different from insects?

2. Can you name two things that spiders can do with their legs?

3. Can you share three other facts about spiders?